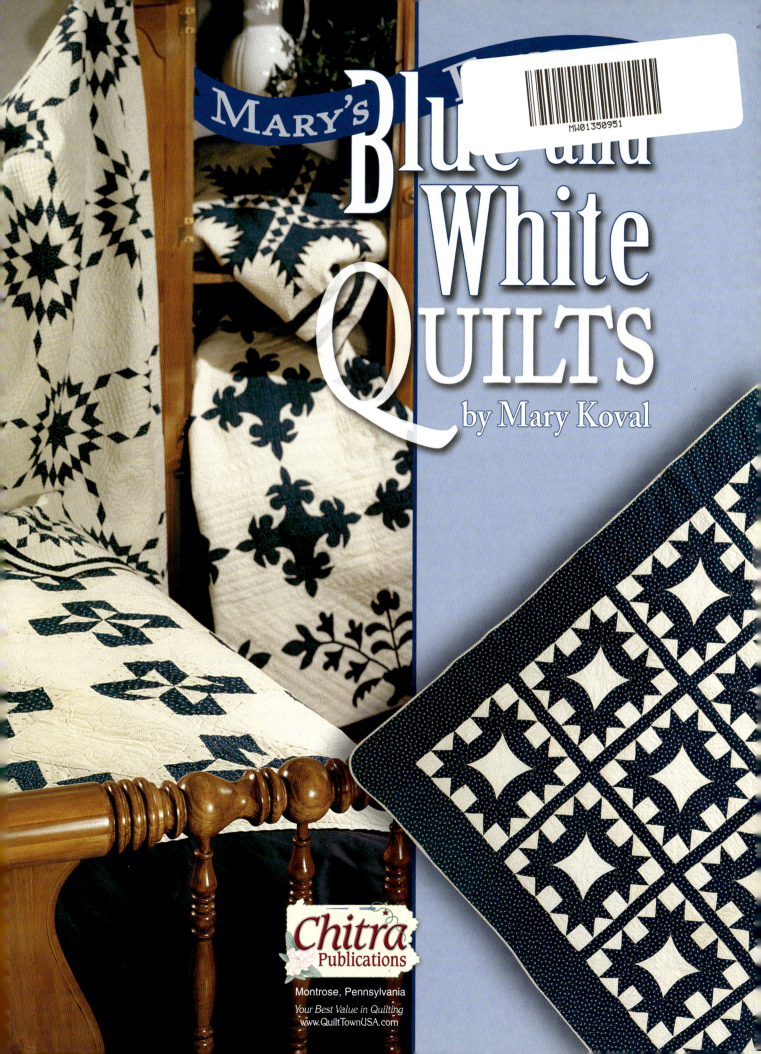

Mary's Blue and White Quilts

by Mary Koval

Chitra Publications
Montrose, Pennsylvania
Your Best Value in Quilting
www.QuiltTownUSA.com

Copyright ©2005 Chitra Publications

All Rights Reserved.
Published in the United States of America.
Printed in China.

Chitra Publications
2 Public Avenue
Montrose, Pennsylvania 18801-1220

No part of this publication may be reproduced or transmitted in any form or by any means, electronic or mechanical, including photocopy, recording, or any information storage and retrieval system now known or to be invented, without permission in writing from the publisher, except by a reviewer who wishes to quote brief passages in connection with a review written for inclusion in a magazine, newspaper, or broadcast.

First Printing: 2005

Library of Congress Cataloging-in-Publication Data
Koval, Mary, 1950-
  Mary's favorite blue & white quilts / by Mary Koval.
    p. cm.
  ISBN 1-885588-65-8 (pbk.)
  1. Patchwork--Patterns. 2. Quilting. 3. Patchwork quilts.
  I. Title: Blue & white quilts. II. Title.
    TT835.K683 2005
    746.46'041--dc22
                            2004030126

Design and Illustrations: Diane Albeck-Grick
Photography: Van Zandbergen Photography, Brackney, Pennsylvania

Our Mission Statement
We publish quality quilting magazines and books that recognize, promote, and inspire self-expression. We are dedicated to serving our customers with respect, kindness, and efficiency.

www.QuiltTownUSA.com

Introduction

When I started collecting antique quilts my husband Joe and I went on many quilt hunts. At the time Joe was not a collector of quilts, but through the years he too gave in to the charm of quilts and began his own collection. I have always admired the originality and craftsmanship of handmade antique quilts while Joe loved the graphic designs.

On one of our quilt hunts in Ohio, we stopped at an antique dealer's home. We bought a few things and were ready to leave when she said, "I have a quilt from my own collection to sell, but it is very expensive. Would you like to see it?" Of course, it cost nothing to look. She brought the quilt into the room with the pattern folded toward the inside. I could tell at a glance this quilt was special. When she opened the quilt, my heart began to pound. It was a blue and white Touching Star (page 28). It touched my heart! This quilt started my love for blue and white quilts. I held it on my lap all the way home to Pennsylvania. That was more than 30 years ago and I still own that quilt! Today, when I take it out of the blanket box I smile as I remember the day I acquired my very first blue and white quilt.

I wrote this book to share with you my love for blue and white antique quilts. Here are a few of my favorites. Enjoy!

My best,

Contents

4 — Delectable Mountains

8 — Feathered Star

10 — Snowball

14 — Odd Fellows Patch

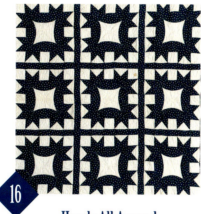
16 — Hands All Around

20 — Fleur de lis

22 — Oak Leaf

26 — Pinwheel

28 — Touching Stars

Delectable Mountains

Quilt Size: 76 1/2" square

Materials
- 4 yards blue print
- 4 yards muslin print
- 4 1/2 yards backing fabric
- 81" square of batting

Cutting

Dimensions include a 1/4" seam allowance.

From the blue print:
- Cut 4: 18 1/4" squares, then cut them in half diagonally to yield 8 triangles (G)
- Cut 2: 16 5/8" squares, then cut them in half diagonally to yield 4 triangles (H)
- Cut 2: 15 1/8" squares, then cut them in half diagonally to yield 4 triangles (B)
- Cut 2: 9 7/8" squares, then cut them in half diagonally to yield 4 triangles (C)
- Cut 56: 6 1/4" squares
- Cut 1: 5" square
- Cut 8: 2 1/8" x 7" strips
- Cut 4: 3" squares, then cut them in half diagonally to yield 8 small triangles

From the muslin:
- Cut 2: 16 5/8" squares, then cut them in half diagonally to yield 4 triangles (F)
- Cut 4: 11 1/8" squares, then cut them in half diagonally to yield 8 triangles (D)
- Cut 2: 9 1/2" squares, then cut them in half diagonally to yield 4 triangles (E)
- Cut 2: 8" squares, then cut them in half diagonally to yield 4 triangles (A)
- Cut 56: 6 1/4" squares
- Cut 8: 1 3/4" x 7" strips
- Cut 6: 3 1/8" squares, then cut them in half diagonally to yield 12 small triangles
- Cut 8: 2 1/2" x 40" strips, for the binding

Directions

1. Draw diagonal lines from corner to corner on the wrong side of each 6 1/4" muslin square. Draw horizontal and vertical lines through the centers.
2. Place a marked muslin square on a 6 1/4" blue square, right sides together. Sew 1/4" away from the diagonal lines on both sides. Make 56.

3. Cut the squares on the drawn lines to yield 448 pieced squares. Press the seam allowances toward the blue print.
4. Lay out 12 pieced squares and the 5" blue square. Sew the squares into sections and sew the sections to the square to make the quilt center.

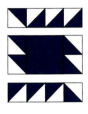

5. Center and sew the muslin A triangles to the sides of the quilt center. The triangles are slightly oversized.

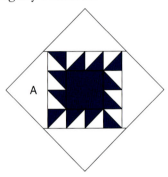

6. Join 6 pieced squares to make a row. Make 4.

7. Lay out the quilt center, the rows, and 4 pieced squares. Sew 2 rows to opposite sides of the quilt center. Sew the pieced squares to the remaining rows and sew the rows to the quilt center.

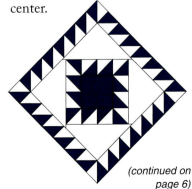

(continued on page 6)

The maker of this 1870's **"Delectable Mountains"** *quilt used what I call "creative piecing." Notice the odd-shaped pieces in some of the sections. They're almost like lightning bolts! The pattern directions have been adjusted so that your quilt will be symmetrical and the pieces will fit.*

Delectable Mountains

(continued from page 4)

8. Center and sew the blue B triangles to the sides of the quilt.

9. Join 12 pieced squares to make a row. Make 4. Sew 2 rows to the quilt. Sew 2 pieced squares to the remaining rows then sew them to the quilt.

10. Join 4 pieced squares then sew them to the side of a blue C triangle. Join 4 pieced squares and a small muslin triangle then sew them to the blue triangle, as shown.

11. Select 16 pieced squares. Trim each one to 2 5/8" square.

12. Join 4 trimmed pieced squares and 2 small blue triangles to make a row, as shown. Make 4.

13. Sew the rows to the remaining side of each triangle.

14. Sew two 1 3/4" x 7" muslin strips to the triangle unit and trim the strip even with the bottom edge, as shown. Make 4.

15. Sew 2 D triangles and an E triangle to a unit, as shown. Make 4. Sew them to the sides of the quilt.

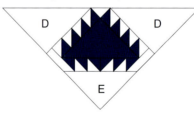

16. Join 20 pieced squares to make a row. Make 4. Sew 2 rows to opposite sides of the quilt. Sew pieced squares to the ends of the remaining rows and sew them to the quilt.

17. Lay out a muslin triangle F, 22 pieced squares, a small blue triangle, and 2 small muslin triangles. Join them to make a triangle unit. Make 4.

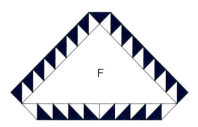

18. Sew the 2 1/8" x 7" blue strips to the triangle units and trim as in Step 14.

19. Sew 2 G triangles and an H triangle to each triangle unit. Sew them to the sides of the quilt.

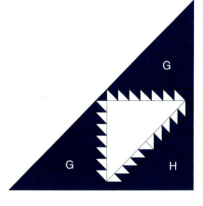

20. Join 32 pieced squares to make a row. Make 4.

21. Sew 2 rows to opposite sides of the quilt. Sew pieced squares to the ends of the remaining rows and sew them to the quilt.

22. Finish the quilt as described in the *General Directions*, using the 2 1/2" x 40" muslin strips for the binding.

✳ Feathered Star ✳

*This is not the **"Feathered Star"** most people recognize. It's unusual in design and technically, the pieces shouldn't fit! The quiltmaker used her skills to "make it work." A few changes have been made to the pattern to ensure that your blocks will go together properly. I have never seen another quilt like this one which I purchased in Lancaster County, Pennsylvania. It was probably made sometime between 1840 and 1850.*

Feathered Star

Quilt Size: 83 1/4" square • Block Size: 23 3/4" square

Materials

- 5 3/4 yards white
- 5 3/4 yards blue print
- 7 1/2 yards backing fabric
- 87" square of batting

Cutting

Dimensions include a 1/4" seam allowance. Cut lengthwise strips before cutting other pieces from the same yardage.

From the white fabric:
- Cut 8: 2" x 88" lengthwise strips
- Cut 9: 12 1/2" squares, then cut them in quarters diagonally to yield 36 large triangles
- Cut 36: 6 3/4" squares
- Cut 36: 4 1/4" squares
- Cut 135: 3" squares, then cut them in quarters diagonally to yield 540 medium triangles
- Cut 54: 1 3/4" squares, then cut them in half diagonally to yield 108 small triangles

From the blue print:
- Cut 8: 2" x 88" lengthwise strips, for the border
- Cut 4: 2 1/2" x 90" lengthwise strips, for the binding
- Cut 9: 10" squares, then cut them in quarters diagonally to yield 36 setting triangles
- Cut 36: 4 5/8" squares, then cut them in half diagonally to yield 72 large triangles
- Cut 36: 4 1/4" squares
- Cut 54: 3" squares, then cut them in quarters diagonally to yield 216 medium triangles
- Cut 9: 2 1/2" squares, then cut them in quarters diagonally to yield 36 small triangles
- Cut 153: 1 3/4" squares

Directions

1. Sew 2 medium white triangles to a 1 3/4" blue square, as shown. Make 99.

2. Lay out 7 pieced sections, 2 medium white triangles, and two 1 3/4" blue print squares. Join them to make a center section, as shown. Make 9. Set them aside.

3. Lay out 2 pieced sections,

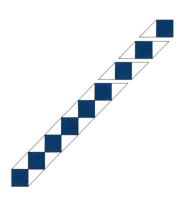

2 medium white triangles, 2 small white triangles, and two 1 3/4" blue print squares. Join them to make a pieced strip, as shown. Make 18.

4. Sew 2 blue setting triangles to a pieced strip to make a unit. Make 18.

5. Sew 2 units to a center section to complete a block center. Make 9. Set them aside.

6. Draw diagonal lines from corner to corner on the wrong side of each 4 1/4" white square.

Draw horizontal and vertical lines through the centers.

7. Place a marked square on a 4 1/4" blue square, right sides together. Sew 1/4" away from the diagonal lines on both sides. Make 36.

8. Cut the squares on the drawn lines to yield 288 pieced squares. Press the seam allowances toward the blue side.

9. Join 3 medium blue triangles, 3 medium white triangles, and a small white triangle to make a strip. Make 36 and 36 reversed, as shown.

10. Select one strip from each group. Sew them to 2 large blue triangles to make a left unit and a right unit, as shown. Make 36 of each.

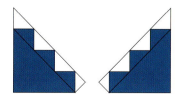

11. Join 4 pieced squares and a medium white triangle to make a strip. Make 36 and 36 reversed, as shown.

12. Select one strip from each group. Sew them to a left unit and a right unit, as shown. Make 36 of each.

13. Lay out a left unit, a right unit, a small blue triangle, and a large white triangle. Sew the blue triangle to the left unit. Sew the white triangle to the right unit. Join the units to make a point section. Make 36.

14. Lay out a block center, 4 point sections, and four 6 3/4" white squares. Sew them into 3 sections and join them to complete a block. Make 9.

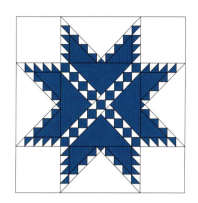

Assembly

1. Sew the blocks into 3 rows of 3. Join the rows.
2. Sew two 2" x 88" blue strips and two 2" x 88" white strips together alternately to make a border. Make 4. Press the seam allowances toward the blue strips.
3. Fold each border in half crosswise and make a mark or place a pin in the border to mark the center.
4. Matching the center of a strip with the center of one side of the quilt, pin the border to the quilt. Sew the border to the quilt, starting and stopping 1/4" from the edges of the quilt top and backstitching.
5. Repeat for the remaining borders.
6. Miter the corners as described in the *General Directions*.
7. Finish the quilt as described in the *General Directions*, using the 2 1/2" x 90" blue strips for the binding.

Snowball

Quilt Size: 72 1/2" x 82 1/2" • Block Size: 10" square

Materials

- 3 1/2 yards blue print
- 5 1/4 yards muslin
- 4 1/2 yards backing fabric
- 77" x 87" piece of batting

Cutting

The patterns (page 12) are full size and include a 1/4" seam allowance, as do all dimensions given. If you prefer to appliqué the curved edges, see Alternate Cutting and Directions on page 12. Cut lengthwise strips before cutting other pieces from the same yardage.

From the muslin:
- Cut 4: 3 3/4" x 78" lengthwise strips
- Cut 21: 10 1/2" squares
- Cut 44: A
- Cut 160: B

From the blue print:
- Cut 4: 3 1/2" x 72" lengthwise strips
- Cut 5: 2 1/2" x 72" lengthwise strips, for the binding
- Cut 40: A
- Cut 176: B

Directions

1. Sew 4 muslin B's to an blue A, as shown. Make 40.

2. Join 4 units to make a block. Make 10.

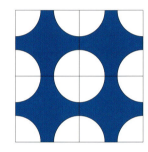

3. Sew 4 blue B's to a muslin A, as shown. Make 44.

4. Join 4 units to make a block. Make 11.

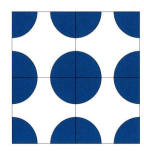

Assembly

1. Referring to the photo, lay out the blocks and 10 1/2" muslin squares. Sew them into rows and join the rows.

2. Measure the length of the quilt. Trim two 3 1/2" x 72" blue strips to that measurement. Sew them to the long sides of the quilt.

3. Measure the width of the quilt, including the borders. Trim the remaining 3 1/2" x 72" blue strips to that measurement. Sew them to the quilt.

4. In the same manner, trim two 3 3/4" x 78" muslin strips to fit the quilt's length and sew them to the long sides of the quilt.

5. Trim the remaining 3 3/4" x 78" muslin strips to fit the quilt's width and sew them to the quilt.

6. Finish the quilt as described in the *General Directions*, using the 2 1/2" x 72" blue strips for the binding.

*I bought this 1870's **"Snowball"** quilt because it's not typical of this design. Generally you'll find Snowball quilts made from 1930's feedsacks so this quilt shows that the pattern is older than some may think. I love this quilt because it's a bit quirky and because it reminds me of Christmas.*

Snowball

Alternate Cutting and Directions for Snowball

To appliqué the curved edges of the snowballs, follow these directions.

1. Cut 5 1/2" squares instead of the A's.

2. Prepare the B's by pressing the curved edges 1/4" toward the wrong side. Appliqué a B to each corner of a 5 1/2" square, aligning the straight edges.

3. Trim the squares behind the B's, leaving a 1/4" seam allowance.

Close-up view

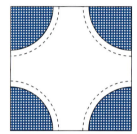

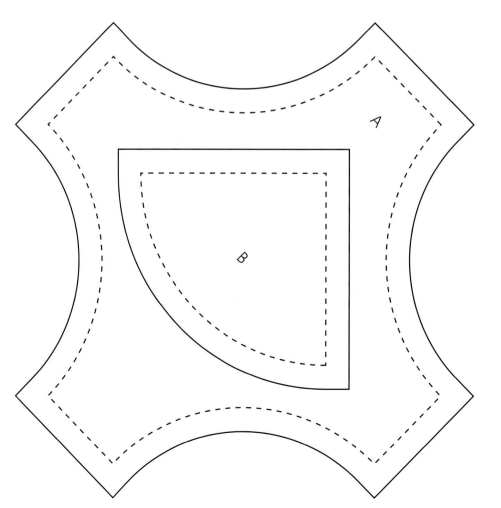

Odd Fellows Patch

In addition to intricate piecing, there is a great deal of hand quilting in this circa 1870's "Odd Fellows Patch." One blue print was used throughout this quilt but you could use assorted blues for a scrappy version.

Odd Fellows Patch

Quilt Size: 88 1/2" square • Block Size: 13 1/2" square

Materials
- 5 1/4 yards blue print
- 7 3/4 yards muslin
- 8 yards backing fabric
- 93" square of batting

Cutting

Dimensions include a 1/4" seam allowance. Cut the lengthwise muslin strips before cutting other pieces from that fabric.

From the muslin:
- Cut 2: 3 1/2" x 86" lengthwise strips
- Cut 2: 3 1/2" x 80" lengthwise strips
- Cut 3: 20 3/8" squares, then cut them in quarters diagonally to yield 12 setting triangles
- Cut 9: 14" squares
- Cut 2: 10 1/2" squares, then cut them in half diagonally to yield 4 corner triangles

From the blue print:
- Cut 10: 2 1/2" x 40" strips, for the binding

For the blocks:

From the blue print:
- Cut 16: 8 3/8" squares, then cut them in quarters diagonally to yield 64 triangles
- Cut 64: 4 3/4" squares
- Cut 192: 1 3/4" x 3" rectangles
- Cut 16: 3" squares
- Cut 64: 2 1/4" squares

From the muslin:
- Cut 384: 1 3/4" squares
- Cut 64: 2 1/8" squares, then cut them in half diagonally to yield 128 triangles
- Cut 64: 4 3/4" squares

For the Sawtooth Borders:

From the blue print:
- Cut 55: 4 3/4" squares

From the muslin:
- Cut 55: 4 3/4" squares

Directions

For the Blocks:

1. Draw a diagonal line from corner to corner on the wrong side of twenty-four 1 3/4" muslin squares.

2. Place a marked square on a 1 3/4" x 3" blue rectangle, right sides together. Sew on the drawn line.

3. Press the square toward the corner, aligning the edges. Trim the seam allowance to 1/4".

4. Place a marked square on the opposite end of the rectangle. Sew on the line. Press and trim as before to complete a Flying Geese unit. Make 12.

5. Sew 2 muslin triangles to a 2 1/4" blue square to make a corner unit, as shown. Press the seam allowances toward the triangles. Make 4.

6. Join 3 Flying Geese units and a corner unit. Make 4.

7. Lay out the pieced units, 4 blue triangles, and a 3" blue square. Sew them into sections and join the sections to complete the block center. Set it aside.

8. Draw diagonal lines from corner to corner on the wrong side of four 4 3/4" muslin squares. Draw horizontal and vertical lines through the centers.

9. Place a marked square on a 4 3/4" blue square, right sides together. Sew 1/4" away from the diagonal lines on both sides.

10. Cut the squares on the drawn lines to yield 32 pieced squares. Press the seam allowances open.

11. Lay out 7 pieced squares and join them to make a row. Make 2.

12. Join 7 pieced squares, reversing the direction, as shown. Make 2.

13. Place the rows next to the block center. Sew the side rows to the block center. Sew the remaining pieced squares to the ends of the top and bottom rows then sew the rows to the block. Make 16 blocks.

Assembly

1. Lay out the blocks, the 14" muslin squares, and the setting and corner triangles. Sew them into diagonal rows and join the rows.

For the borders:

1. Make 440 pieced squares as described in Steps 8 through 10, using fifty-five 4 3/4" muslin squares and fifty-five 4 3/4" blue squares.

2. Join 51 pieced squares as shown in Step 11 of the Block Directions to make a border. Make 2. Sew them to opposite sides of the quilt.

3. Join 51 pieced squares, reversing the direction as shown in Step 12. Make 2. Referring to the photo, sew a pieced square to each end of the borders. Sew the borders to the remaining sides of the quilt.

4. Sew the 3 1/2" x 80" muslin strips to opposite sides of the quilt.

5. Sew the 3 1/2" x 86" muslin strips to the remaining sides.

6. Join 57 pieced squares to make a border as in Step 2. Make 2. Sew them to opposite sides of the quilt.

7. Join 57 pieced squares to make a border as in Step 3. Make 2. Sew a pieced square to each end of the borders. Sew the borders to the remaining sides of the quilt.

8. Finish the quilt as described in the *General Directions*, using the 2 1/2" x 40" blue strips for the binding.

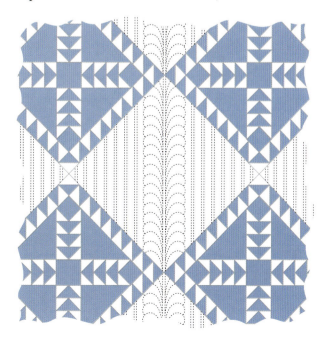

Hands All Around

Quilt Size: 63 3/4" x 77 1/4" • Block Size: 12 3/8" square

Materials

- 5 yards blue print
- 2 1/4 yards muslin
- 3/4 yard shirting print for the binding
- 4 3/4 yards backing fabric
- 68" x 81" piece of batting

Cutting

The patterns (page 18) are full size and include a 1/4" seam allowance as do all dimensions given. Cut all strips on the lengthwise grain before cutting other pieces from the same fabric.

From the blue print:
- Cut 4: 6" x 68" strips
- Cut 4: 1 3/4" x 55" strips
- Cut 19: 2" x 52" strips, then cut 17 diamonds from each strip

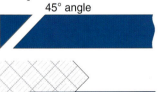

- Cut 15: 1 3/4" x 12 3/4" strips
- Cut 80: B

From the muslin:
- Cut 160: 2 5/8" squares
- Cut 40: 4 1/4" squares, then cut them in quarters diagonally to yield 160 triangles
- Cut 20: A

From the shirting print:
- Cut 8: 2 1/2" x 40" strips, for the binding

Directions

1. Sew a 2 5/8" muslin square to a blue B, backstitching at each seamline, as shown. Make 4.

2. Sew a unit to each side of a muslin A to make the block center. Set it aside.

3. Sew 2 diamonds together, as shown, stopping and backstitching at the seamline, as before. Make 8.

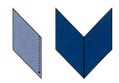

4. Set a muslin triangle into each pair of diamonds.

5. Join 2 diamond units, backstitching at the seamline.

6. Set a muslin square into the unit. Make 4.

7. Set the units into the block center to complete the block. Make 20.

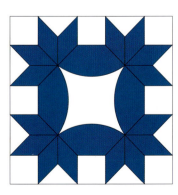

(continued on page 18)

"Hands All Around," *circa 1870, also known as All Hands Round, Old Fashioned Star, and Wreath of Lilies, was hand pieced in the late 1800's. The directions and templates given are for machine piecing for the intermediate to advanced quilter.*

Hands All Around

(continued from page 16)

Assembly

1. Sew 4 blocks and three 1 3/4" x 12 3/4" blue strips together alternately to make a row. Make 5.
2. Measure the length of the rows. Trim the 1 3/4" x 55" blue strips to that measurement.
3. Sew the block rows and trimmed strips together alternately.
4. Measure the length of the quilt. Trim two 6" x 68" blue strips to that measurement. Sew them to the sides of the quilt.
5. Measure the width of the quilt, including the borders. Trim the remaining 6" x 68" blue strips to that measurement. Sew them to the top and bottom of the quilt.
6. Finish the quilt as described in the *General Directions*, using the 2 1/2" x 40" shirting print strips for the binding.

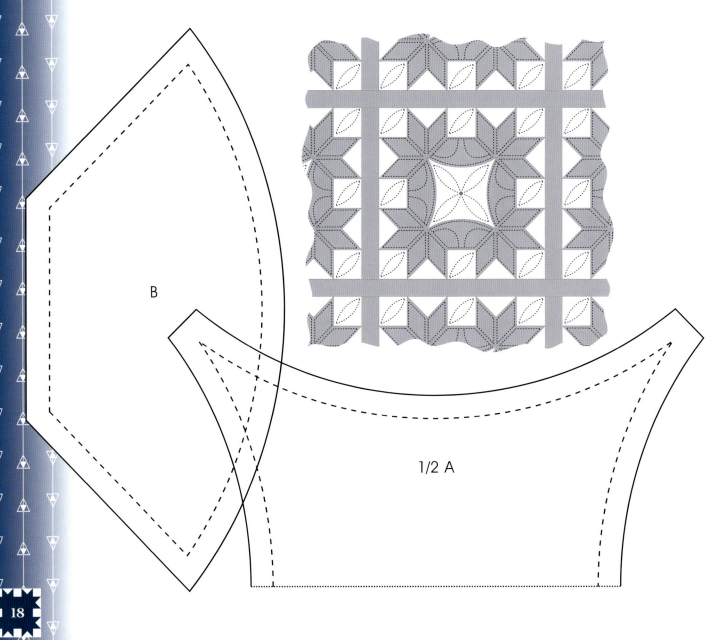

Fleur de lis

I purchased this quilt because I love the border. **"Fleur de lis"** *was made about 1860. Its maker hand stitched her quilt very heavily with decorative quilting such as a feather design in the plain blocks and diagonal lines in sets of three on the borders.*

Fleur de lis

Quilt Size: 84 1/2" square • Block Size: 10" square

Materials

- 7 yards white
- 4 yards blue print
- 7 3/4 yards backing fabric
- 89" square of batting

Cutting

The appliqué patterns (pages 21 and 25) are full size and do not include a seam allowance. Make a template from each pattern. Trace around the templates on the right side of the fabric and add a 1/8" to 3/16" turn-under allowance as you cut the pieces out. All other dimensions include a 1/4" seam allowance. Cut lengthwise strips before cutting other pieces from the same yardage.

From the white fabric:
- Cut 2: 14 1/2" x 86" lengthwise strips
- Cut 2: 14 1/2" x 58" lengthwise strips
- Cut 3: 15 1/2" squares, then cut them in quarters diagonally to yield 12 setting triangles
- Cut 16: 11" squares
- Cut 9: 10 1/2" squares
- Cut 2: 8" squares, then cut them in half diagonally to yield 4 corner triangles

From the blue print:
- Cut 5: 2 1/2" x 73" lengthwise strips, for the binding
- Cut 16: A
- Cut 10: B
- Cut 10: C
- Cut 20: D
- Cut 20 and 20 reversed: E
- Cut 40 and 40 reversed: F
- Cut 10 and 10 reversed: G
- Cut 20: 3/4" x 10" bias strips
- Cut 10: 3/4" x 6 3/4" bias strips

Directions

1. Center and pin an blue A on an 11" white square. Appliqué the A to the square, turning under the edges as you stitch. Make 16.
2. Press the blocks on the wrong side.
3. Trim each block to 10 1/2" square, keeping the appliqué centered.

For the borders:
1. Fold a 14 1/2" x 58" white strip in half crosswise and press the fold. Measure 14 1/8" from the crease on both sides and press to make creases.

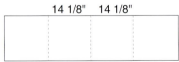

2. Press the long edges of the 3/4"-wide bias strips 1/4" toward the wrong side.
3. Referring to the photo, pin or baste an urn (B) and a 6 3/4" bias strip over each outer crease. Pin or baste the 10" bias strips and the remaining pieces in place. Be sure to keep the pieces 1" from the long edges of the border strip and 1 1/2" from the ends.
4. Appliqué the pieces to complete a border. Make 2.
5. Fold a 14 1/2" x 86" white strip in half and press the fold. Measure 28" from the crease on both sides and press to make creases.
6. Pin or baste the appropriate appliqué pieces on the strip, using the creases for placement. Appliqué the pieces in place to complete a border. Make 2.

Assembly

1. Lay out the blocks, squares, and setting and corner triangles. Sew them into diagonal rows and join the rows.
2. Measure the width of the quilt. Trim the short borders to that measurement if necessary. Sew them to opposite sides of the quilt.
3. Measure the quilt including the borders. Trim the long borders to that measurement, if necessary, and sew them to the quilt.
4. Finish the quilt as described in the *General Directions*, using the 2 1/2" x 73" blue strips for the binding.

Oak Leaf

Quilt Size: 72" x 90" • Block Size: 18" square

Materials
- 5 1/2 yards white
- 5 yards blue print
- 5 1/2 yards backing fabric
- 76" x 94" piece of batting

Cutting
The appliqué patterns (page 24) do not include a seam allowance. Make a template from each pattern. Trace around the templates on the right side of the fabric and add a 1/8" to 3/16" turn-under allowance when cutting the pieces out. Cut lengthwise strips before cutting other pieces from the same fabric. All other dimensions include a 1/4" seam allowance.

From the white fabric:
- Cut 12: 19" squares
- Cut 4: 9 1/2" x 75" lengthwise strips, for the borders

From the blue print fabric:
- Cut 84: small leaves
- Cut 48: large leaves
- Cut 12: flowers
- Cut 1 1/2"-wide bias strips, totaling at least 450" when joined end to end
- Cut 9: 2 1/2" x 40" strips, for the binding

Directions
For each of 12 blocks:

1. Fold a 19" square in quarters and press the folds.

2. Fold the pressed square in quarters diagonally. Press.

3. Using the creases as guidelines, baste a flower in the middle of the square.

4. Referring to the quilt photo, baste four small leaves on the vertical and horizontal creases and four large leaves on the diagonal creases, tucking the stems under the center design.

5. Needleturn appliqué the pieces in this order: small leaves, large leaves, and the flower. Make 12.

6. Trim the blocks to 18 1/2" square, keeping the appliqué centered.

Assembly

1. Lay out the blocks in 4 rows of 3. Stitch the blocks into rows and join the rows.

2. Measure the length of the quilt. Trim two 9 1/2" x 75" white strips to that measurement and stitch them to the long sides of the quilt.

3. Measure the width of the quilt, including the borders. Trim the remaining 9 1/2" x 75" strips to that measurement and stitch them to the top and bottom of the quilt.

4. Press the long edges of the blue print bias strip 1/4" toward the wrong side.

5. Referring to the photo for placement, baste the winding vine and the remaining small leaves to the border, being sure the stems are tucked under the vine.

6. Appliqué the leaves then the vine.

7. Finish the quilt as described in the *General Directions*, using the 2 1/2" x 40" blue print strips for the binding.

Setting a goal of gathering 100 blue and white quilts for a book, I acquired 25 before becoming intrigued by a red and green quilt. In order to diversify my collection, I needed to sell some blue and white quilts. Parting with **"Oak Leaf"**, *circa 1880, was difficult.*

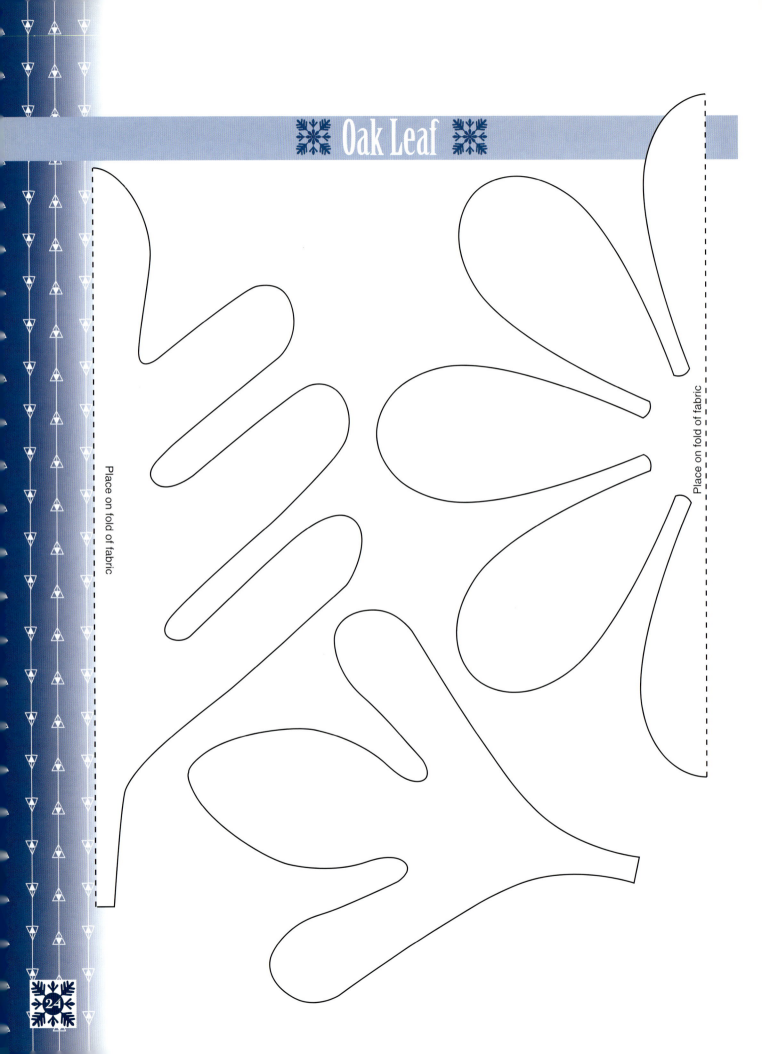

Pinwheel

Quilt Size: 85" square • Block Size: 10" square

Materials

- 2 3/4 yards blue print or several prints totaling at least 3 yards
- 2 3/4 yards white shirting print
- 6 1/2 yards muslin
- 7 5/8 yards backing fabric
- 89" square of batting

Cutting

Dimensions include a 1/4" seam allowance.

From the blue print:
- Cut 18: 6 3/4" squares
- Cut 36: 6 1/4" squares, then cut them in quarters diagonally to yield 144 large triangles
- Cut 72: 3 3/8" squares, then cut them in half diagonally to yield 144 small triangles

From the shirting print:
- Cut 18: 6 3/4" squares
- Cut 36: 6 1/4" squares, then cut them in quarters diagonally to yield 144 large triangles
- Cut 72: 3 3/8" squares, then cut them in half diagonally to yield 144 small triangles

From the muslin:
NOTE: *Cut the lengthwise strips before cutting squares.*
- Cut 2: 2 1/2" x 180" lengthwise strips, for the binding
- Cut 5: 15 1/2" squares, then cut them in quarters diagonally to yield 20 setting triangles
- Cut 25: 10 1/2" squares
- Cut 2: 8" squares, then cut them in half diagonally to yield 4 corner triangles

Directions

1. Draw diagonal lines from corner to corner on the wrong side of each 6 3/4" shirting square. Draw horizontal and vertical lines through the centers.

2. Place a marked square on a 6 3/4" blue square, right sides together. Sew 1/4" away from the diagonal lines on both sides. Make 18.

3. Cut the squares on the drawn lines to yield 144 pieced squares. Press the seam allowances toward the blue print.

4. Lay out 4 pieced squares in either of the following arrangements, and join them to make a pinwheel. Make 36. Set them aside.

5. Sew 2 small blue triangles to a large shirting triangle. Make 72. Set them aside.

6. Sew 2 large blue triangles to a large shirting triangle.

7. Sew 2 small shirting triangles to the ends, as shown. Make 72.

8. Lay out a pinwheel and 4 pieced sections, as shown. Join them to make a block. Make 36.

Assembly

1. Lay out the blocks, 10 1/2" muslin squares, and the muslin setting and corner triangles.

2. Sew the blocks, squares, and triangles into diagonal rows. Join the rows.

3. Finish the quilt as described in the *General Directions*, using the 2 1/2" x 180" muslin strips for the binding.

*This "**Pinwheel**" design is sometimes called The Colorado Quilt. Made about 1890, it comes from Blair County, Pennsylvania. The quilting is simple with one flower-like design in the plain blocks and a second one in the pieced blocks.*

Touching Stars

Quilt Size: 78" square • Block Size: 14 3/8" square

Materials

- 6 yards white
- 4 1/2 yards blue print
- 4 3/4 yards backing fabric
- 82" square of batting

Cutting

Dimensions include a 1/4" seam allowance. Cut pieces in the order listed.

From the white fabric:
- Cut 4: 2" x 80" lengthwise strips, for the border
- Cut 40: 1 1/2" x 52" lengthwise strips
- Cut 25: 7 5/8" squares, then cut them in quarters diagonally to yield 100 triangles
- Cut 100: 5" squares

From the blue print:
- Cut 4: 2 1/2" x 84" lengthwise strips, for the binding
- Cut 4: 2" x 77" lengthwise strips, for the border
- Cut 50: 1 1/2" x 52" lengthwise strips

Directions

1. Sew two 1 1/2" x 52" blue strips to a 1 1/2" x 52" white strip to make a panel, as shown. Make 20. Press the seam allowances toward the blue strips.

2. Trim the left end of each panel at a 45° angle, as shown.

3. Cut twenty 1 1/2" sections from each panel. Check the angle between cuts and trim if necessary to maintain a 45° angle.

4. Sew two 1 1/2" x 52" white strips to a 1 1/2" x 52" blue strip to make a panel. Make 10. Press the seam allowances toward the blue strips.

5. Trim the left end of each panel, as before.

6. Cut twenty 1 1/2" sections from each panel.

7. Join 2 sections from the first group and one from the second to make a star point, as shown. Make 200.

8. Join 2 star points, backstitching at the 1/4" seamlines. Set a 5" square into the star point unit. The squares are slightly oversized. Make 100.

10. Join 4 units to make a star. Set 4 white triangles into the sides of the star to complete a block. Make 25.

11. Trim the edges 1/4" beyond the star points to square the blocks.

(continued on page 30)

My collection of blue and white quilts started with **"Touching Stars"**, *an 1870's treasure I purchased in Montgomery County, Ohio. Not wanting to put this quilt down, I carried it home on my lap in the car. I especially like the way the quiltmaker quilted concentric circles only 1/4" apart over the star blocks. She also quilted feathered circles in the plain squares. The quilt design for the feathered circle is on page 31.*

Touching Stars

(continued from page 28)

Assembly

1. Lay out the blocks in 5 rows of 5. Sew them into rows and join the rows.
2. Measure the length of the quilt. Trim two 2" x 77" blue strips to that measurement. Sew them to opposite sides of the quilt.
3. Measure the width of the quilt, including the borders. Trim the remaining 2" x 77" blue strips to that measurement. Sew them to the remaining sides of the quilt.
4. In the same manner, trim two 2" x 80" white strips to fit the quilt's length. Sew them to the quilt.
5. Trim the remaining 2" x 80" white strips to fit the quilt's width and sew them to the quilt.
6. Finish the quilt as described in the *General Directions*, using the 2 1/2" x 84" blue strips for the binding.

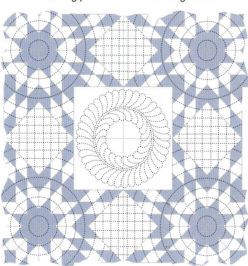

Quilting placement for Touching Stars

Quilting placement for Feathered Star

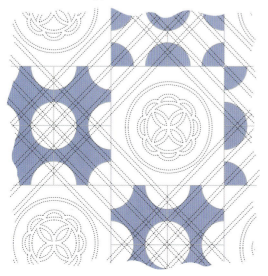

Quilting placement for Snowball

Quilting placement for Pinwheel

General Directions

About the Patterns

Read through the pattern directions before cutting fabric. Pattern directions are given in step-by-step order. Batting and backing dimensions for the quilts include 4" extra beyond the finished size of the quilt top.

Fabrics

We suggest using 100% cotton. Wash fabric in warm water with mild detergent. Do not use fabric softener. Dry fabric on a warm-to-hot setting. Press with a hot dry iron to remove any wrinkles.

Piecing

For machine piecing, sew 12 stitches per inch, exactly 1/4" from the edge of the fabric, unless instructed to do otherwise in the pattern. Start and stop stitching at the cut edges, unless instructed to do otherwise in the pattern.

For hand piecing, begin with a small backstitch. Continue with a small running stitch, backstitching every 3-4 stitches. Stitch directly on the marked line from point to point, not edge to edge. Finish with 2 or 3 small backstitches before cutting the thread.

Appliqué

Appliqué pieces can be stitched by hand or machine. To hand appliqué, baste or pin the pieces to the background in stitching order. Turn the edges under with your needle as you appliqué the pieces in place. Do not turn under or stitch edges that will be overlapped by other pieces. Finish the edges of fusible appliqué pieces with a blanket stitch made either by hand or machine.

To machine appliqué, baste pieces in place close to the edges. Then stitch over the basting with a short, wide satin stitch using a piece of tear-away stabilizer under the background fabric. You can also turn the edges of appliqué pieces under as for needleturn appliqué, and stitch them in place with a blind-hem stitch.

Mitered Borders

Miter the corners in the following way: With the quilt top right side down, lay one border over the other. Using a pencil, draw a straight line at a 45° angle from the inner to the outer corners.

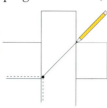

Reverse the positions of the borders and mark another corner-to-corner line. With the borders right sides together and the marked seamlines carefully matched, stitch from the inner seamline to the outer corner, backstitching at each end. Open the mitered seam to make sure it lies flat, then trim the excess fabric and press. Repeat for the remaining corners.

Finishing Your Quilt • Marking Quilting Designs

Mark before basting the quilt top together with the batting and backing. Chalk pencils show well on dark fabrics, otherwise use a very hard (#3 or #4) pencil or other marker for this purpose. Test your marker first.

Basting

Cut the batting and backing at least 4" larger than the quilt top. Tape the backing, wrong side up, on a flat surface to anchor it. Smooth the batting on top, followed by the quilt top, right side up. For hand quilting, baste the three layers together in a grid of lines 6" apart. For machine quilting, pin the layers with safety pins 5-6" apart.

Binding

To make 1/2" finished binding, cut 2 1/2"-wide strips. Sew strips together with diagonal seams; trim and press seam allowances open.

Fold the strip in half lengthwise, wrong side in, and press. Position the strip on the right side of the quilt top, aligning the raw edges of the binding with the edge of the quilt top. Leaving 6" of the binding strip free and beginning a few inches from one corner, stitch the binding to the quilt with a 1/4" seam allowance measuring from the raw edge of the quilt top. When you reach a corner, stop stitching 1/4" from the edge of the quilt top and backstitch. Clip the threads and remove the quilt from the machine. Fold the binding up and away from the quilt, forming a 45° angle, as shown.

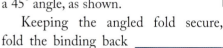

Keeping the angled fold secure, fold the binding back down. This fold should be even with the edge of the quilt top. Begin stitching at the fold.

Continue stitching around the quilt in this manner to within 6" of the starting point. To finish, fold both strips back along the edge of the quilt so that the folded edges meet about 3" from both lines of stitching and the binding lies flat on the quilt. Finger press to crease the folds. Measure the width of the folded binding. Cut the strips that distance beyond the folds. (In this case 1 1/4" beyond the folds.)

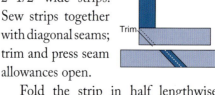

Open both strips and place the ends at right angles to each other, right sides together. Fold the bulk of the quilt out of your way. Join the strips with a diagonal seam, as shown.

Trim the seam allowance to 1/4" and press it open. Refold the strip, wrong side in. Place the binding flat against the quilt, and finish stitching it to the quilt. Trim excess batting and backing so that the binding edge will be filled with batting when you fold the binding to the back of the quilt. Blindstitch the binding to the back, covering the seamline.